VOLCANO
SURVIVAL STORIES

BY AMY C. REA

childsworld.com

ABOUT THE AUTHOR

Amy C. Rea is the author of several children's books. She also writes about travel and food in Minnesota. She lives in Saint Anthony, Minnesota, with her husband and silly dog.

The Child's World
childsworld.com

Published by The Child's World®
800-599-READ • www.childsworld.com

Photography Credits
Photographs ©: Dicky Bisinglasi/AP Images, cover, 1; Shutterstock Images, 5, 6, 22, 24; Jack Smith/AP Images, 8; Rob Crandall/Shutterstock Images, 10; Carlos Osorio/AP Images, 12; Desislava Antonova/Shutterstock Images, 15; iStockphoto, 16; Bardocz Peter/Shutterstock Images, 18; Fredy Thuerig/Shutterstock Images, 19; US Geological Survey/AP Images, 20; Michael Schade/AP Images, 25; New Zealand Police/AP Images, 26; Red Line Editorial, 28 (Antarctica), 28–29

ISBN Information
9781503854567 (Reinforced Library Binding)
9781503854796 (Portable Document Format)
9781503855175 (Online Multi-user eBook)
9781503855557 (Electronic Publication)

LCCN 2023937093

Printed in the United States of America

BRINGING THE WORLD TO YOUNG READERS 1968

CONTENTS

WHAT IS A VOLCANO?

Volcanoes are **vents** in Earth's surface. There are three different types of volcanoes. A cinder cone looks like a hill with a **crater** on top. Another type is a composite volcano, or stratovolcano. These volcanic mountains can reach more than 8,000 feet (2,440 m) tall. Shield volcanoes have a gradual slope and are wide, sometimes stretching for miles.

Very hot, melted rock can be found underneath a volcano. This is known as magma. When a volcano **erupts**, it releases magma, steam, and rocks. Magma is called lava once it hits Earth's surface. During an eruption, lava may pour out of a volcano or shoot into the air. Some volcanoes are constantly erupting. Others stay inactive for hundreds of years.

The United States has about 160 active volcanoes, many of which are located on the West Coast, in Hawaii, and in Alaska. The strong blast during an eruption can hurt people nearby. People can get **severe** burns. Breathing in volcanic ash may hurt people's lungs. Volcanic eruptions can also cause other issues, such as mudslides and wildfires.

FAST FACTS

- Mount St. Helens in Washington erupted on May 18, 1980. It killed 57 people.
- On November 13, 1985, the Nevado del Ruiz volcano erupted in Colombia. It caused deadly mudslides that left more than 23,000 people dead.
- Kilauea is on Hawaii's Big Island. Between May and August of 2018, lava poured onto the southeastern part of the island. The lava flow ruined more than 700 homes. Thousands of people had to flee the area, but no one died.
- On December 9, 2019, 47 people were visiting White Island, also known as Whakaari. This active volcano is off New Zealand's coast. The volcanic eruption killed 22 people.

CHAPTER ONE

MOUNT ST. HELENS

It was May 18, 1980. Venus Dergan and Roald Reitan were asleep in a tent by the Toutle River in Washington State. They had set up camp 30 miles (48 km) away from Mount St. Helens. When they fell asleep, all they heard was the breeze in the trees.

◀ **The 1980 Mount St. Helens eruption was one of the most powerful eruptions in North America's recorded history.**

They could hear the gentle gurgling of water nearby. But in the early morning, Dergan woke up to the sound of a siren.

The couple looked outside their tent, wondering what was going on. Then they noticed the river. The day before, the water had been quiet and gentle. Now, the water roared and rushed forward. Something was terribly wrong. But they did not know what it was.

Not knowing why the river had changed so much was frightening. Dergan and Reitan gathered their belongings and ran to their car. The river continued to rise and moved toward them. Dergan and Reitan wanted to drive away as fast as they could, but their car would not start. They were stuck.

The couple didn't know it yet, but a large, muddy-looking mass called a lahar was moving down the river toward them. A lahar, or volcanic mudflow, sometimes forms when a volcano erupts. This happens when the eruption melts ice and snow. Lahars are a mix of water, ash, rocks, and ice. They can reach speeds of up to 50 miles per hour (80 kmh). When a lahar reaches a river, it can cause the river to travel much faster than normal.

Upstream was a train **trestle**. It had mud and **debris** piled up against it. When the lahar hit the trestle, it loosened the debris.

▲ **Mudslides and flash floods from the eruption pushed objects, such as logs, into rivers and backed them up.**

Dergan and Reitan saw the debris-filled river rush toward them. At that moment, they knew they were in danger. They yelled at each other to get on top of the car. They scrambled to the roof just as the mud and debris surrounded the vehicle. The mud picked up the car and pulled it along. Dergan and Reitan fell into the river, which was now four times larger than it had been the night before.

The river's force was strong, making it impossible to swim to safety. Reitan reached out and grabbed Dergan. He pulled her near a log that was rushing down the river. Together they held onto the piece of wood. "The man saved my life," said Dergan. "I will always be forever grateful to him."

TIMELINE: THE ERUPTION OF MOUNT ST. HELENS

Many events happened around the time of the Mount St. Helens eruption.

MARCH 16, 1980

A series of small earthquakes are the first signals of activity at Mount St. Helens.

MARCH 27

Mount St. Helens erupts for the first time in more than 100 years. The explosions of steam blast through the mountain's icy summit.

APRIL 1

Columns of steam and ash soar 20,000 feet (6,100 m) into the sky.

MAY 7–17

More eruptions begin on May 7 and last for ten days.

MAY 18

An earthquake triggers a massive landslide. Within minutes, the debris travels at more than 300 miles per hour (480 kmh). Nearly all the trees are destroyed within 6 miles (9.7 km) around the volcano. Lava begins to come out of the volcano. Lahars form and rush down the mountain.

Dergan and Reitan were swept approximately 1 mile (1.6 km) down the river before they could escape and get back to dry ground. They still did not know what had happened or if anyone would find or help them.

Later that day, a helicopter spotted Dergan and Reitan and brought them on board. It was then that the couple finally learned Mount St. Helens had erupted. The siren they had heard that morning was a warning to **evacuate**.

"We were lucky that we got out of the tent when we did," Dergan said. "They probably would never have found us. We would have been buried alive."

◀ **The volcano's blast was so powerful that it blew up the top of the volcano, leaving behind a crater.**

CHAPTER TWO

SWEPT AWAY

Fernando Diaz and his family lived in Armero, Colombia. They'd had a strange couple of days. Ash from the nearby Nevado del Ruiz volcano fell the night of November 12, 1985. At 6:00 p.m. the next day, a fire truck drove through the town. Someone inside the truck was speaking through a loudspeaker.

◀ **The lahars hit Armero, Colombia, about two hours after the Nevado del Ruiz volcano exploded. They swept away many buildings.**

The person was telling everyone to stay home. The person said they should not panic, so Diaz and his family went to bed.

Later that night, Nevado del Ruiz erupted. Giant lahars brought a wall of mud and melted ice water into the town at high speeds. Diaz woke to a roaring, grinding noise. It was hard to see outside in the dark. He went to the front door to look out, but the door would not open. The water and mud had blocked his door shut.

FIVE DEADLIEST VOLCANOES

The Nevado del Ruiz eruption was one of the worst volcanic eruptions in modern history.

Where and When	Deaths	Top Cause of Deaths
Tambora, Indonesia (1815)	92,000	Starvation after ash in the sky led to a volcanic winter and crops couldn't grow
Krakatau, Indonesia (1883)	Around 36,000	Tsunami, or a large and powerful wave, caused by the volcano's eruption
Mount Pelée, Martinique (1902)	Around 30,000	Hot flows that included lava, gases, and ash
Nevado del Ruiz, Colombia (1985)	More than 23,000	Mudslides
Unzendake, Japan (1792)	Between 14,000 and 15,000	Tsunami and the volcano collapsing

Diaz went to the second floor of the house, opened a window, and started to climb out. He got caught in a roaring flood of mud. It began carrying him away. He did not know if his family was OK.

Eventually, the mud rammed Diaz into something solid. He could feel the ground under his knees. He was at a hill. He began to climb as best he could. The more of his body he pulled out of the mud, the faster he could go. All around him, Diaz heard people crying and shouting. Still, he felt very alone. "I could hear everybody crying for help, but no one came," he said.

The lahar finally began to slow down. The roar quieted. Dim light appeared in the east as the sun rose, barely visible through the ash and steam from the volcano. The town was covered in 15 feet (4.6 m) of mud. About 30,000 people lived in Armero before the volcano erupted. More than 23,000 people were killed because of the eruption.

Diaz tried to search for his family, but he couldn't find them. The only thing he could do was go to Bogotá, Colombia. Some of his other family members lived there. It was 60 miles (97 km) away. Heartbroken and hurting all over, Diaz left his destroyed town.

Records suggest that Nevado del Ruiz erupted in 1595. It erupted again in 1845 and 1985. ▶

CHAPTER THREE

LAVA AT THE FRONT DOOR

It was March 2018, and the Kilauea volcano on Hawaii's Big Island was spewing lava in two separate areas. This wasn't necessarily a cause for worry—the volcano had been doing this for almost ten years. The top of the volcano even had a lava lake. But by the middle of the month, experts noticed something different about the volcano. The magma beneath it had a spike in pressure.

On April 30, one area of the volcano collapsed. Two days later, the lava lake started to drain and move underground. Earthquakes followed. Starting on May 3, the ground began cracking open approximately 25 miles (40 km) from the top of the volcano, in a neighborhood called Leilani Estates. At first, only steam came out of the cracks. But then hot lava began spewing out.

◄ **Kilauea is one of Earth's most active volcanoes.**

Hawaii County government officials ordered people in Leilani Estates to evacuate. Heath Dalton lived there. On May 4, Dalton grabbed his suitcase and began shoving items into it. He paused to look out a window. He saw a crack in the ground only a block away. Then a roaring sound filled the air. It reminded Dalton of a jet engine. Red, hot lava began exploding out of the crack. Dalton frantically grabbed whatever belongings he could and fled the neighborhood, hoping to outrun the lava.

HAWAII'S ACTIVE VOLCANOES

Hawaii's islands are made from many volcanoes. In fact, the islands are part of a chain of volcanoes that extends across the Pacific Ocean. Six of Hawaii's volcanoes are active.

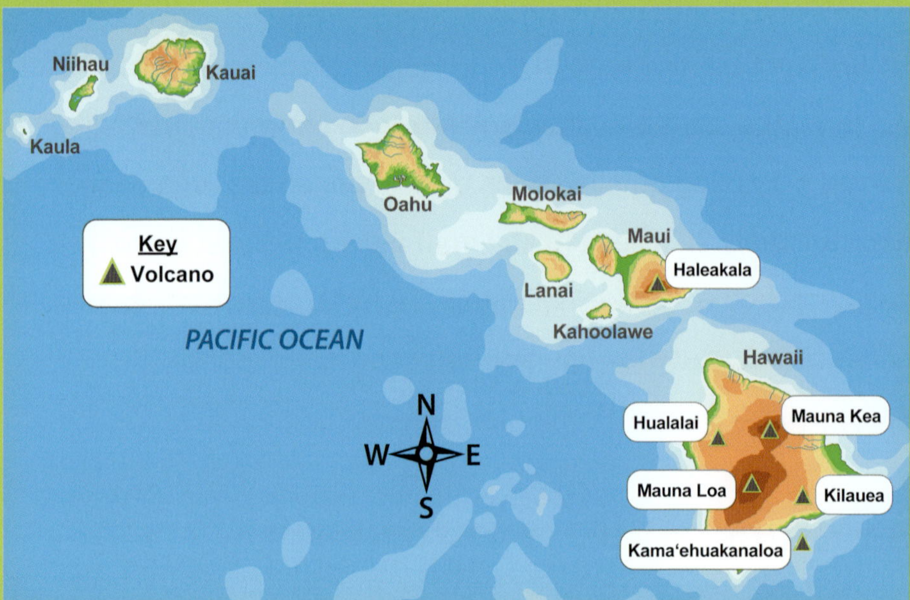

▲ **Many cracks opened in the ground during the 2018 eruption. The most notable was called Fissure 8. It spewed a large amount of lava.**

The next day, Dalton was upset. There were so many important belongings in his house that he wanted to save. He mustered the courage to go back home. As Dalton approached his neighborhood, he could see dark smoke rising into the air. Then he saw bright-orange flames. His house was on fire. Dalton turned around and headed for a safer place.

Talmadge Magno worked for the county. His job was to help people during natural disasters. Magno knew that some people were not taking the evacuation order seriously. He could see smoke and ash pouring into the sky from the volcano. Worse, he saw a tall pile of lava and bright-yellow flames moving down Makamae Street toward people's homes.

▲ **Rivers of lava changed Hawaii's landscape.**

Reports came in that some people were not leaving the area. They thought they would be safe even as the lava continued to spread. Magno knew this was not true. So government workers headed to Leilani Estates. They visited houses and banged on the doors. If people answered, the workers begged them to leave.

People close enough to the lava could feel the heat coming from it. The lava had cooled a little since leaving the volcano, but could still be as much as 2,085 degrees Fahrenheit (1,141°C). If people touched or came into contact with the lava, it would leave horrible burns on their skin. The lava would destroy anything in its path.

"Kind of disturbingly, some people just refused to leave," said Magno. "We had one gentleman that had to be kind of rescued. His only way out was through his back door and through the forest."

No one died from the Kilauea volcano eruption, but it still disrupted many people's lives. Magno knew his job was dangerous. But he was proud of his work and happy to save people. "Sometimes you go, 'Am I cut out for this?' But you have to understand that there's going to be some really rough days," Magno said in an interview. He said the best part of his job is knowing he has helped people. "A passion I find in emergency response is supporting the community, our state, our country. That's the reward," he said.

CHAPTER FOUR

TRAPPED TOURISTS

It was December 9, 2019. Stephanie Browitt, her dad, and her sister were on a cruise ship. The boat cut through the deep blue water toward a mass of rock jutting out of the ocean. The group was ready to tour White Island, or Whakaari. This was a volcano off the North Island of New Zealand.

◄ **Tours to White Island stopped after the 2019 eruption.**

White smoke rose from the volcano. Once they were on the island, the tour guides made a surprising announcement: the volcano was showing more signs of activity than usual. In fact, it had been for weeks. This meant there was a higher chance of an eruption. "I was a little concerned," said Browitt. "But at the same time you sort of have trust that we wouldn't be on here, they wouldn't be running tours if they thought it was dangerous."

Browitt and her family began their hike to the volcano's crater. They paused for a picture upon reaching it. Browitt had been on the island for around 30 minutes when the white smoke turned black behind her. A tour guide she was with yelled, "Run!"

Everyone began scrambling away from the crater. A roar from the volcano filled the air. Rocks, thrown up from the volcano's blast, slammed into the ground around them. People yelled in terror. The force from the volcano pushed Browitt to the ground. She could feel her body burning. "I didn't think I would survive. . . . It was the most terrifying moment of my life," Browitt said.

She saw that others around her were forced to the ground, too. People were crying. Browitt couldn't see her dad or sister anywhere. Moving was difficult. Ash filled the air, and the warm sun beat down on her. Browitt's whole body was in pain.

Then Browitt heard her dad's voice. He called her name, and she yelled back to him. Browitt remained on the hard, hot ground for almost an hour. The volcano rumbled beneath her, and she was terrified that there would be another eruption.

PARTS OF A VOLCANO

Volcanoes can be very different from each other, but they all have two features in common. First, they all have vents. Second, they have pathways from the vents to the magma.

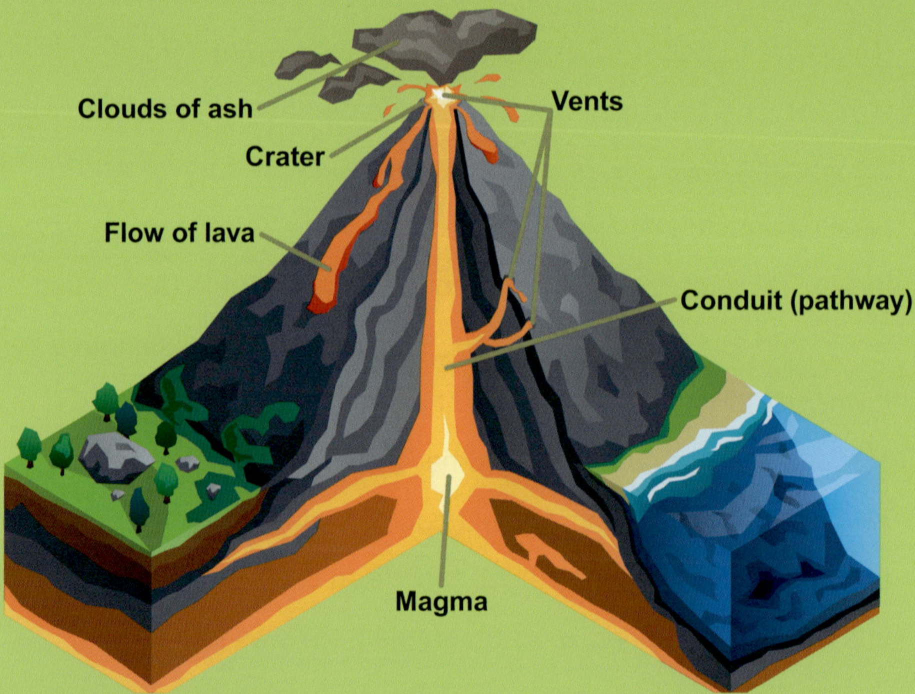

▲ **People on a nearby boat saw and photographed the eruption.**

Then the sound of helicopter blades joined the grumbling volcano. Pilots landed and began looking for survivors. One of them found Browitt's dad and tried to help him, but he begged the pilot to take Browitt to safety first. So Browitt was carefully placed in the helicopter with four other injured people. It took 20 minutes to fly back to the mainland. Once there, Browitt was rushed to the hospital. Her burns were life-threatening and covered around 70 percent of her skin. She lost the tops of her fingers. Her father was brought to the hospital, too, but he later died from his injuries. Browitt never found out exactly what happened to her sister. All she knew was that her sister didn't survive.

▲ **Police divers looked for bodies in the water after the eruption.**

Healing from severe burns is a slow and painful process. Browitt had several **operations**. Her skin was burned too badly to grow back. People donated pieces of their own skin to be put onto Browitt's body to replace her burned skin.

Browitt had to wear special wrappings called compression bandages for months. These bandages helped her burn scars heal, so that they would not be as bad as they would have been if left alone. But Browitt knew her body and face would still look different than they did before. She was lucky to be alive and to have her mom, who hadn't been on the volcano when it erupted. Browitt had gone to the island with 47 people, and 22 of them died. "I'm grateful for mum, that I can be here for her and she can be here for me, that we have each other," Browitt said.

THINK ABOUT IT

- Would you be interested in exploring a volcano? Why or why not?
- Imagine you are near a volcano and are told to leave the area immediately. What would you do and why?
- How can you help someone who has lost everything to a volcanic eruption?

VOLCANO MAP

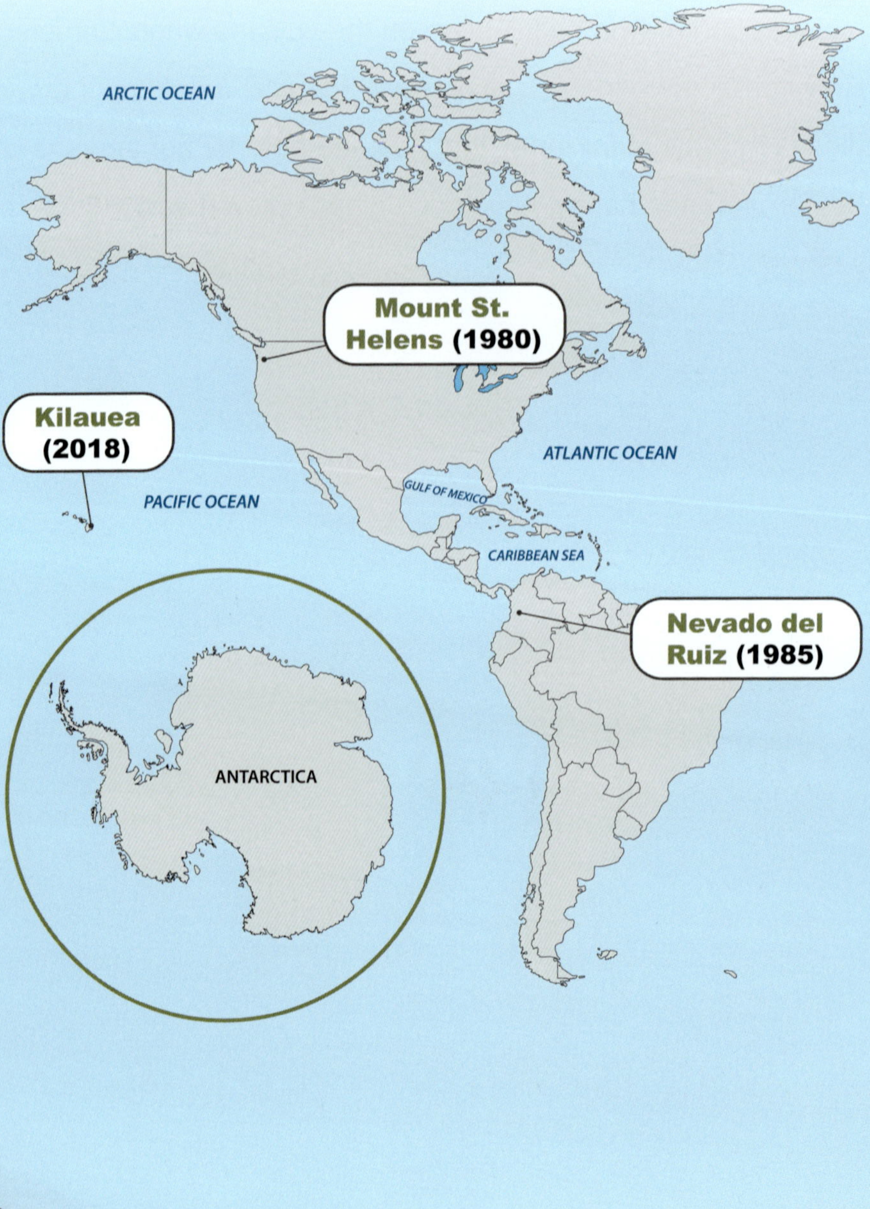
ARCTIC OCEAN
Mount St. Helens (1980)
Kilauea (2018)
ATLANTIC OCEAN
GULF OF MEXICO
PACIFIC OCEAN
CARIBBEAN SEA
Nevado del Ruiz (1985)
ANTARCTICA

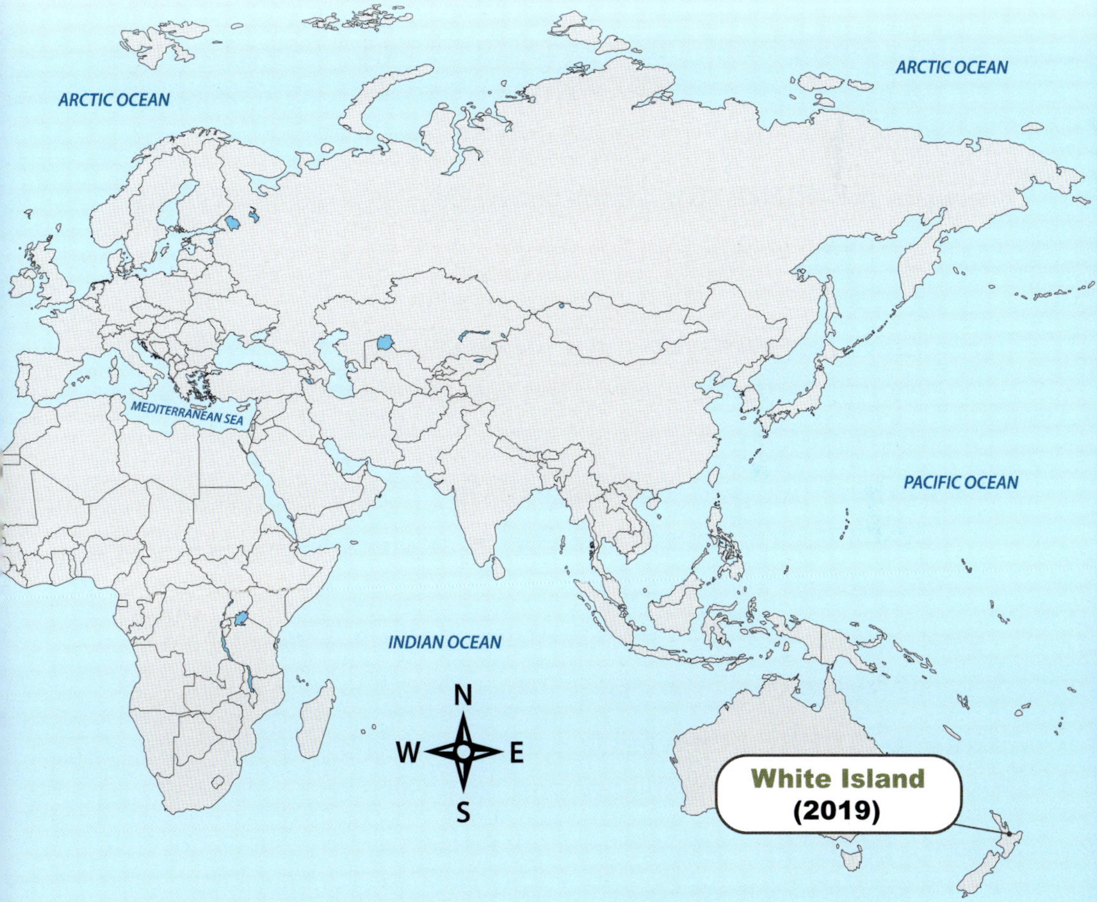
ARCTIC OCEAN
ARCTIC OCEAN
MEDITERRANEAN SEA
PACIFIC OCEAN
INDIAN OCEAN
N
W
E
S
White Island
(2019)

GLOSSARY

crater (KRAY-tur): A crater is a large dip on the side or top of a volcano, usually right above the vent from which lava and other materials come out during an eruption. Lava poured from the crater.

debris (duh-BREE): Debris is made up of pieces of things that have been destroyed or broken down. The debris from the volcano was found miles away.

erupts (eh-RUHPTS): If a volcano erupts, it is pushing out things such as steam and lava. It is dangerous for people to be near a volcano when it erupts.

evacuate (eh-VAK-yoo-ayt): To evacuate means to leave a dangerous area immediately. The people were told to evacuate the area around the volcano.

operations (ah-puh-RAY-shuns): Operations are procedures done by doctors to mend an injured person. She had to have many operations to treat her burns.

severe (suh-VEER): Something that is severe is worse or more painful than usual. Her injuries from the eruption were severe.

trestle (TREH-sell): A trestle is a framework that helps hold up a bridge. The debris piled up against the trestle.

vents (VENTS): Vents are openings that allow gases, steam, or lava to escape. There was steam shooting out of the vents at the top of the volcano.

SELECTED BIBLIOGRAPHY

"About Volcanoes." *USGS*, n.d., usgs.gov. Accessed 25 Apr. 2023.

"Key Facts about Volcanic Eruptions." *Centers for Disease Control and Prevention*, 25 Jan. 2022, cdc.gov. Accessed 25 Apr. 2023.

"2018 Eruption and Summit Collapse." *NPS*, 7 June 2021, nps.gov. Accessed 25 Apr. 2023.

FIND OUT MORE

BOOKS

Farndon, John. *Extreme Volcanoes.* Minneapolis, MN: Hungry Tomato, 2017.

Nargi, Lela. *Volcanoes.* Washington, DC: National Geographic, 2018.

Romero, Libby. *All about Volcanoes.* New York, NY: Children's Press, 2021.

WEBSITES

Visit our website for links about volcanoes:
childsworld.com/links

Note to Parents, Caregivers, Teachers, and Librarians: We routinely verify our Web links to make sure they are safe and active sites. So encourage your readers to check them out!

INDEX